Utrillo

Maurice Utrillo at work

Utrillo

TEXT BY

WALDEMAR GEORGE

80 ILLUSTRATIONS

WITH 35 IN COLOR

NEW YORK GRAPHIC SOCIETY

GREENWICH, CONNECTICUT

LIBRARY OF CONGRESS CATALOG CARD NUMBER 60-10474 - LITERARY AND REPRODUCTION RIGHTS RESERVED FOR ALL COUNTRIES

© COPYRIGHT 1960 IN ITALY BY SILVANA EDITORIALE D'ARTE - MILAN-ITALY

PRINTED IN ITALY

Prologue

Utrillo became a legend in his own lifetime: biographies of him are all, or nearly all, *vies romancées* and even his origins are shrouded in mystery. Is he the son, as Tabarant states, of the former journalist Boissy or of Miguel Utrillo who gave him his name and from whom, according to Carco, Utrillo may have inherited his almost Moorish, certainly Spanish cast of feature?[1] Alcoholism is not the key to Utrillo's genius, nor does his hereditary background enable us to understand him. The vocation of most painters declares itself spontaneously but Utrillo began to paint only because he was made to. Art, of which his mother taught him the rudiments, was at first simply a means of therapy. Suzanne Valadon's doctor advised her to give the boy a definite objective on which to concentrate. He might thus just as easily have become a locksmith or cabinet maker. People have wondered if Utrillo's work is the expression of a certain social level at a given time and in a given place. Analogies with Impressionism or with the Dutch period of Van Gogh are too superficial to be taken into consideration. There is no link between the painter of Montmartre and the patriarch of Eragny (Pissarro) or the wandering pastor of the Borinage. His parentage is still obscure and Suzanne Valadon herself has referred to the matter in rather evasive terms. His real antecedents are those popular masters whom art historians persist in underrating. Utrillo, who created marvels with the patience of a commercial artist, is akin to those obscure decorative painters of the nineteenth century who illustrated the walls of little inns in the Ile-de-France and were probably the last real heirs of an authentic secular tradition. Utrillo's greatness cannot be separated from his humility. His townscapes have been put on the same level as those of Corot or Vermeer. But such comparisons are usually arbitrary and in this case irrelevant.

After 1917 (or 1916) Utrillo reverted to a sort of "vernacular" style. But his crudeness, far from standing in the way of his creating masterpieces, gave his pictures a quality of directness and beauty of structure. Is it possible to say that this infant prodigy never underwent the influence of an aesthetic or intel-

---

(1) Mme. Lucie Valore, Utrillo's widow, claims Utrillo was the son of Puvis de Chavannes, which information she claims to have obtained from Suzanne Valadon.

Montmagny landscape (*charcoal drawing*)

lectual milieu? No one has yet pointed out the similarity between his own vision and that of a peculiarly Parisian novelist such as Céline. *Voyage au bout de la nuit* makes a direct appeal to the visual intelligence of the reader. A canvas by Utrillo might almost be said to be the pictorial equivalent.

Utrillo was probably attracted by the work of Armand Guillaumin, who, about the time when Utrillo was a boy, was considered—more than Sisley or Camille Pissarro—to be a faithful and objective painter of working class districts. Finally, Utrillo's youthful technique, his scribbles, his outlines traced with an illiterate hand which is already deceptive, ally him, however strange this may seem, with those sorcerer's apprentices: the pre-war Cubists who tried to put painting back on its feet by considering it as a form of manual dexterity.

Life

Many writers have already given accounts of the pathetic story of Utrillo's life, but it is again necessary to consider these episodes as they form a background to an art which is wholly spontaneous. The boy who was one day to be called Maurice Utrillo was born on the 26th December, 1883. He was registered in the name of his mother Marie-Clémentine (later Suzanne) Valadon. This former acrobat who lived in Montmartre had the opportunity of meeting artists, and of visiting the studios of masters who were already famous. She posed for Puvis de Chavannes. She appears in his *Bois Sacré*, a Greek nymph translated into Gothic terms. She was Renoir's model for *La Danse à la Ville*, and its pendant, *La Danse à la Campagne*. She managed to attract the irascible painter of *Les Jeunes Spartiates*—Degas—who encouraged her to draw and gave her a few lessons. The outstanding draughtsman of the century taught this tight-rope walker, Suzanne Valadon, and her clear and incisive sketches reveal the influence of the master. Amateur painter and hard-working model, Suzanne Valadon was not able to look after her son personally; she entrusted him to Mme Coulon and he grew up in the company of this simple-hearted woman. He was a thin-faced boy with delicate features and a precocious intelligence, uncommunicative and disturbingly highly-strung,

Maurice Utrillo and his wife Lucie Valore with their dogs in the garden of their villa at Le Vésinet

who gave his foster mother a great deal of worry. Taciturn and easily angered, he had obsessions. His pursuits and pleasures were not normal for a boy of his age. He joined his mother in the studio in which she lived and worked in the rue de Tourlaque. He learned to read and write in a school in the rue Doudeauville, in the 18th arrondissement. The Institution Flaisselle was not a free state school but a private establishment. Although his school life was bourgeois his family background was composed of artists. When Suzanne Valadon became the mistress and subsequently the wife of M. Paul Mousis, agent for a well-known trading company, Maurice followed her to Pierrefitte. Paul Mousis, who accepted the presence of his young wife's son, steadfastly refused to give him his name. On the 8th April, 1891 Maurice was recognised by Miguel Utrillo y Molins, born in Barcelona on the 16th February, 1863. Miguel Utrillo, painter, architect, essayist, man of taste and patron of the arts, was artistic adviser to the Barcelona magnate Plandiura. Maurice, who never met him, lived with his mother, Paul Mousis and Mme. Coulon in a big house surrounded by a garden, not far from Montmagny.

Until the summer of his tenth year Maurice attended the local school. Then he became a day boy at a secondary school in Paris, where he went every day by train. Paul Mousis considered that he was providing an education suitable for a boy of good family. But Maurice found new friends and came home late, often after having stopped at a few cafés on the way, and his mother's reproaches had no effect. Nevertheless, he was a gifted and intelligent scholar. His headmaster made him concentrate on mathematics and he won prizes for arithmetic for several years in succession. But he had no perseverance and he never attained his certificate of studies.

Paul Mousis, disappointed and worried, found the boy a position in a banking house. To begin with he gave great satisfaction with his work on the book-keeping side, but his touchy wayward temperament went against him. He made fun of his superiors and answered them back impertinently. He was dismissed and returned to Pierrefitte, with no trade or profession. Bored and restless he squandered his overflowing energy in the dance-halls of Montmagny. Mme. Coulon and Suzanne Valadon misguidedly put their savings at his disposal and he spent everything on drink. His conduct was judged scandalous, yet it was probably no more so than that of many rich and spoilt young people whose exploits daily receive more indulgent treatment from the press than any of

Utrillo's biographers have seen fit to mete out. Was drink alone the cause of his unruliness? Or was he, on the other hand, a sick man who tried to forget his misery in the oblivion of alcohol? So far these questions have remained unanswered. The tradition of the artist or writer who brings about his own destruction, and a literature coloured by romanticism have obscured the judgment of contemporary biographers. Too many writers have found it more lucrative to exaggerate the unhappy artist's conflicts with the forces of order than to assess objectively the cause of his actions. The theory that "genius is akin to madness" lends credibility to these stories: what clairvoyant or psycho-analyst will throw a beam of light on the sickness that undermined the body of this visionary obsessed with bad dreams?

Scandal succeeded scandal. Suzanne Valadon, spurred on by her husband, took her 18-year-old son to Dr. Vallon who had him admitted to the psychiatric hospital of Sainte-Anne. Medical treatment proved successful. Apparently cured and relieved of his alcoholic cravings, Maurice soon returned to Pierrefitte. In spite of his boredom, he appeared to lead an exemplary life. He lived in the open air and went for long walks. He discovered the countryside. He came home before nightfall and went early to bed. But this period of calm did not last long. Suzanne then consulted Dr. Ettlinger. This enlightened man advised her to deliver her son from the increasing burden of his neurosis by giving him pencils, brushes and a paint-box.

"I who am weak in front of life, lean on my sister," said Cézanne to Vollard. Utrillo, who was also weak, painted to kill time and to please the mother whom he loved tenderly. Seated before his easel, he forced himself to copy faithfully the landscape he could see from his window. His behaviour was that of a medium. His palette, reduced to five colours, was made up for him by Suzanne Valadon. He worked like a diligent pupil and his mother soon realised that he had a good eye. She was surprised by the quality of her son's efforts and decided that he should have drawing lessons. Maurice sulked, but submitted. He was nineteen years old and feeling his way. Could he find his salvation in a task that would free him from nightmares and enable him to express himself fully? The doctors who had him under observation permitted him to go out alone. He went to Paris, and, with an emotion which he did not bother to hide, found his way back to Montmartre where he was born and which was to be the scene of his future exploits. In 1903 his age-group was

The Ferry (*charcoal drawing*)

called up for military service but Maurice was not accepted. He was temporarily deferred.

The pace began to quicken. Utrillo now lived with his mother in Paris, in the rue Cortot. He painted regularly but had no thoughts of selling. Paul Mousis supplied their needs. For the moment he knew nothing of the poverty that Van Gogh and Modigliani were forced to suffer. Until 1909, when his mother separated from her first husband, his life was secure. After that it became more precarious. He paid for the glasses of wine that he drank at the bar by offering his canvases in exchange. Some drove him away, others gave him credit. Others exploited his weakness and bartered drink for his pictures. His physical decline coincided with the full flowering of his childish yet impressive art. He broke mirrors, insulted policemen and pursued pregnant women for whom he had a particular aversion. Decent people shunned him. He picked up companions who made him drunk, beat him up, then left him speechless at a street corner. He was taken home with his clothes in ribbons and his face swollen. He was looked after and locked in his room, but managed to slip past his guards, get hold of the forbidden drink, sketch a picture or two and take to the streets once more. The destructive cycle had begun again. He painted furiously. In 1903-4 he painted 50 pictures and the early part of the white period included more than 600 canvases! But although he exhibited in the Salon des Indépendants and the Salon d'Automne, after 1909 his contacts with other artists were rare. This solitary lived away from the herd.

According to Tabarant, the frame-maker Anzoli was Utrillo's first dealer. He was succeeded by Serat, Jacobi, Level, Soulier and Sagot. With the exception of Level and Sagot, all were junk dealers. In 1909, Libaude came into the artist's life. He immediately realised his worth, bought one of his pictures and tried to buy him up by offering him 500 francs for ten canvases, and as a last resort, assured for himself the right to a first option on the artist's entire output for a monthly sum. This rarely surpassed 300 francs. The eventual disagreement between Utrillo and his manager has been the subject of various comments; there is no doubt that the artist was exploited, many artists are until they are famous. Libaude at least deserves the credit of preserving the artist's most important works. When these were sold at auction and then exhibited at the Galerie Hodebert in 1928, public opinion realised that France possessed a great painter.

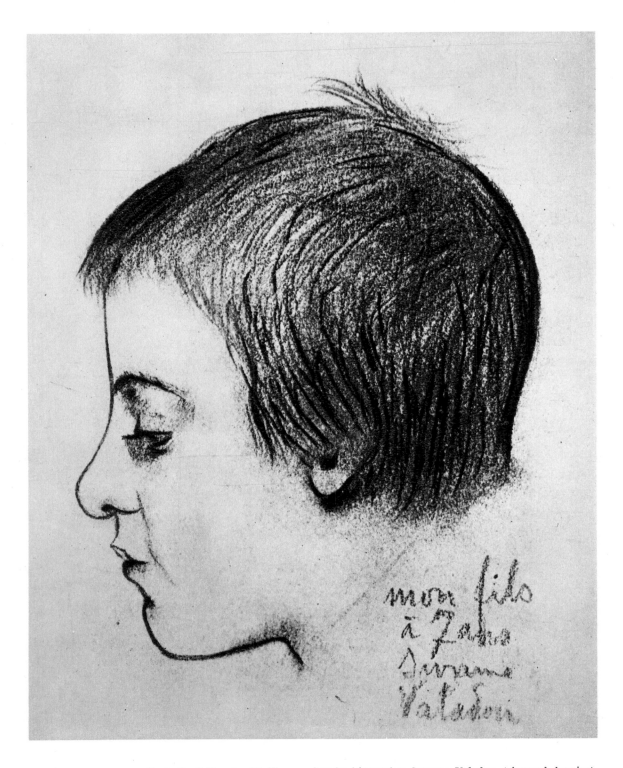

Portrait of Maurice Utrillo as a boy by his mother Suzanne Valadon (*charcoal drawing*)

In 1910, after an attack of delirium tremens, Utrillo was admitted to the clinic at Sannois. Here he was looked after with intelligence and good will. The doors of the clinic were never closed; the artist could walk out, could paint in the open air if he wished and after two months' treatment he was given an exit permit and went to Brittany and Corsica. Although his arrangement with Libaude did not come to an end until 1914, he signed up in the meantime with M. Marseille, then returned to Libaude who staged his first exhibition at the Galerie Eugène Blot in the rue Richepanse (26th May - 9th June, 1913). Utrillo had other opportunities for placing his works. The café proprietors Gay and Marie Vizier welcomed him warmly, offered him hospitality with no thought of anything in return, advanced him money and sold his pictures. At Gay's "Casse-Croûte," at Marie Vizier's "Belle Gabrielle," he had a room where he could work and sleep. Wine flowed freely. And at the "Casse-Croûte," where kind-hearted M. Gay kept him company when he painted between bouts of drinking, Maurice Utrillo wrote his Memoirs which have never seen the light of day. The manuscript of "The Autobiography of Maurice Utrillo, Landscape Painter" today belongs to M. Pétridès. And in the back room of the café proprietor who became his follower and whose pictures had a certain success, Utrillo painted the café "A la Belle Gabrielle" which bears this inscription: "Facing you is the happiest memory of my life." He loved Marie Vizier tenderly. Was this love returned? One day Utrillo had the bizarre but touching idea of decorating the lady's lavatory. When Marie Vizier went in, the paint was still wet. She hastened to remove it from the wall!

At the beginning of the war, Utrillo was called up but was subsequently released. He returned to Montmartre, his pockets empty and with his dealers away at the front. He sold off his brilliant but barely negotiable canvases. Suzanne Valadon left Paris to join her second husband, the painter André Utter who was mobilised in a town near the front. Utrillo's wandering life began again, his places of refuge were the bars of M. Gay and Marie Vizier. In 1916 he entered the hospital of Villejuif and was put with the insane. He lived in a nightmare and reacted by painting in secret his first pictures in violent colours. After a few months he left the asylum and in 1917 underwent further treatment in a clinic at Picups, with Leopold Zborowski paying his fees. This picture dealer and symbolist poet of Polish origin also helped Modigliani and Soutine before dying a poor man in 1932. In 1918 Utrillo entered yet another

14

Suzanne Valadon. Portrait of Maurice Utrillo aged 20 (*charcoal drawing*)

clinic for nervous disorders at Aulnay-sous-Bois. He escaped and took refuge with M. Gay who hid him in a room. He handed his host this note, dated 6th September: "I promise not to go out before the end of September." A few days later, he disappeared.

After the war, Paris began to discover Utrillo. The prices of his pictures followed a steady upward curve. His exhibition at the Galerie Lepoultre in 1919 was a moral and material success such as his first admirers could not have foreseen. The painter could have drawn some profit from this situation, but fate had yet another blow in store for him. Once again he was put in a psychiatric clinic. But this time his name was known and his work sought after, his new guardians supplied him with painting materials, made him drink and encouraged him to work. They confiscated his pictures in the hope of selling them and allowed him to escape in order to cover up a scandal from which they might have expected the worst consequences. Back now with his mother, under surveillance, Utrillo was only allowed out with a nurse who was also his bodyguard. In 1929 he was arrested on a charge of indecent behaviour outside the Bourse. Beaten up by the police and jeered at by the crowd, he was condemned to six days imprisonment.

The man was persecuted, the painter adulated. He was made the subject of books and articles. The Galerie Bernheim-Jeune offered him a contract which he consented to sign, but his already tragic life was to continue in the same vein.

There was a further attack after which he spent some time in the clinic at Ivry and then returned to the rue Cortot where he painted and played with an electric train. One day he got over the wall. Police brought him back home with a fractured jaw. After a few weeks rest, he left by car for the old château de Saint-Bernard which had been bought by Suzanne Valadon and Utter. There he underwent a long convalescence. Pictures by Utrillo hung in public galleries all over the world but the captive existence which he led in the sumptuous house in the Avenue Junot belonging to his mother and her second husband, did nothing to help his sickness. Between attacks, he worked, prayed, sang old songs and went through his souvenirs. In 1934 he married Mme. Lucie Valore who installed him in a fine villa in Le Vésinet, looked after his affairs and watched over his health. He was decorated by Edouard Herriot who personally pinned on Utrillo's breast the Cross of a Chevalier de la Légion d'Honneur. After the second World War he rarely appeared in public, although he was present at a retrospective of Suzanne Valadon's work (she died in 1938). Paul Pétridès became his sole agent, his apartment in the rue Delcassé houses an outstanding collection of Utrillo's works. Maurice Utrillo died in Dax on the 16th November, 1955. His body was brought back to Paris and his tomb can be seen in the cemetery of Montmartre, in the shadow of the Sacré-Cœur, the barley-sugar church that inspired so many masterpieces.

Work

The chronology of Utrillo's work presents certain problems. After 1925-30, the artist abandoned any form of logical research. He painted from memory, returned to subjects he had treated previously or went back to his earliest attempts. Certain snow scenes painted after the second World War might almost be dated 1918. The only difference is that the handling is more summary, perhaps more mechanical. In the main, Utrillo's work falls into four periods. It is generally held that the painter of Montmartre began under the influence of the Impressionists, Pissarro and Sisley, whose works he could have seen in the Salle Caillebotte (Musée du Luxembourg) or in Durand-Ruel's gallery or Tanguy's shop. This point of view is arguable. Utrillo's earliest works are opaque and dark in colour, worked with the brush like oil sketches by Jongkind. There is no trace of an Impressionist palette.

The popular basis of Utrillo's art is barely visible in his early works. This adolescent was no working painter covering crumbling walls with his hieroglyphics. His mother, whose art is brutal but by no means unsophisticated, had worked with Degas, Lautrec and Renoir. She had revealed her powers in the unofficial Salons and exhibited in the galleries. Unlike the Douanier Rousseau, she did not admire official artists who, in her opinion, painted smoothly, deceived the eye, were members of the Institut de France and were invited to soirées at the Elysée.

"Utrillo had practically no education," wrote Francis Carco. This is unlikely because we know he remained at school (the Collège Rollin) until he

17

Cabaret (*brush drawing*)

was sixteen. He read a great deal. He was particularly fond, says Tabarant, of popular scientific works. Before it became clouded over, his mind was lively. Having grown up in Paris in an artistic atmosphere, Utrillo could not be in total ignorance of the work of contemporary painters, as he has proved by his reference to Sisley. The style of his letters denotes a learning that is by no means inferior to that of the greater number of artists of his time and we know that he wrote verse. Utrillo, whose mature works are like votive pictures (in a profane sense) with their roots in folklore, started to paint at the age of twenty, like many other young bourgeois. His pictures were not in the least like prints, a supposedly minor art form, nor could one find any signs of that innocence which was to become so marked later on and which was his own particular trade mark. His pictorial material gradually acquired the depth which it lacked. His palette was composed of five colours; zinc-white, two yellows, vermilion and rose madder; he normally painted on cardboard, because it was more flexible than canvas on a stretcher. He worked rapidly; in one or two sittings the painting was finished. He sketched in the general composition of his picture with charcoal and a ruler. His technique, which has been called pre-Impressionist, reached its apogee in 1905-6. But the surface of *Notre-Dame pavoisée* (14th July, 1908) is still dotted and streaked with colour. The sky, the trees, the water, the bridge over the river and the almost fluid mass of buildings are composed of some light and indefinite substance. The forms seem to spring from a network of irregular brush-strokes. Although he does not have recourse to complementary colours, the artist shows in this superb work a manual dexterity which verges on virtuosity. The paintings of the Montmagny period are muddy and heavily impasted. At the same time, Utrillo produced paintings where an occasional deep colour is put on as if with a trowel. Inscriptions begin to appear; so do figures. These are swallowed up in the picture space; they have no separate life. They are small and discreet. They are rendered so schematically that it is not possible to identify them. Dreary and almost deserted streets... because Utrillo is a town painter. His rigorous perspectives, despite their air of poverty, remind one of Florentine and Sienese landscapes of the Quattrocento. Haunting in their banality, the façades of the houses are pierced with a hundred windows, and each window seems to be watching and hiding the story of a life. These views of Paris, whose scenery is reduced to a few anaemic trees, reveal the hopelessness peculiar to great cities. And yet Utrillo paints

19

them with love, he is the child of an exclusively urban tradition. The grey stone city is his favourite setting... the white period, which began in 1907 or 1908, lasted until the beginning of the 1914 war. Utrillo's palette then became lighter; a few clear colours were added. He modelled in flat shapes and his planes, indicated with a fairly crude mixture of plaster and glue, have the grain of rough cast walls. Figures, which had disappeared, came back towards 1910 and became more precise. The comic silhouettes of working class women, so like puppets, stand out more clearly against their concrete background. His drawing became tighter. The colours, acid and dry, became thicker. Utrillo, the painter of Paris, ranges the city of which he is the consummate chronicler. Whether painting from life or from picture post-cards, his subjects are the same; the streets of Montmartre with cafés indicated by signs; quiet little squares, as quiet as those of provincial towns; Sacré-Cœur, one of his leit-motifs, the Lapin Agile, a country inn with its white fence; the deserted Moulin de la Galette, and those dingy barracks which, as he paints them, look like prisons.

But the white period was not confined to Parisian subjects. There were a considerable number of paintings of Brittany and Corsica which are far from being landscapes in their natural state. Utrillo is feeling his way. He found it in architecture, however mediocre this may appear. He magnified an ordinary wall with crumbling cement, a Swiss chalet built in Seine-et-Marne, a nineteenth century Gothic cathedral...

Utrillo's churches form an immense rosary. In 1929 they numbered nearly seventy. After Saint-Denis and Notre-Dame, those repositories of the history of France, the artist painted, in 1914, the cathedral in which the Kings of France were crowned. The fire of Rheims, the cathedral destroyed by enemy bombs, inspired an ex voto which bears comparison with the visions of Patinir and El Greco. Utrillo painted many pictures of Notre-Dame. But he also painted Saint-Severin, Saint-Nicholas-des-Champs, the churches of Clignancourt and Clichy, Lourdes, (which looks like an architectural joke) Chartres, Moulins, Saint-Malo. Some of these places of prayer and contemplation are painted in cold artistry. Others are acts of faith, for example Notre-Dame is a hymn to the glory of God. The most sumptuous churches as well as the iron chapels of the suburbs represent steps on Utrillo's road to salvation. Is it true to say that the first works that reveal the extent of his genius as a colourist date from his confinement at Villejuif, in August 1916? These brilliantly coloured paintings could be consid-

"Le Lapin Agile" (*pencil sketch*)

ered as compensations. They prove that Utrillo was never mad or that his will triumphed over his weaknesses. It is probable that these works are earlier than his wartime stay in the sinister asylum on the Seine.

In his later works the range of his colours widens. We are told that at this time he abandoned the palette that his mother had imposed on him. This is possible, but Utrillo was never so close to Suzanne Valadon as at this time. His methods were never simpler. He lost all feeling for oil paint and one has the impression that he is working in tempera. His houses, built out of shoddy materials, are covered with cheap tiles, the grandiose expressionism of his cathedrals, constructed from slate, clay and mud, belongs to the past, as does the luminous whiteness of his landscapes, like illuminated manuscripts by Jean Fouquet or the brothers Limbourg. There begins to emerge a style with qualities of childishness that it is barely possible to overlook, and it should be understood that the idea of childishness is not necessarily a bad thing when applied to works of an aesthetic nature. In art, childishness can be a source of renewal and an element of regeneration.

A selection of landscapes peopled by female figures with hind-quarters like brood mares was exhibited in Berthe Weill's gallery in the rue Laffitte in 1918. They were recent works which the painter referred to in a letter written from the lugubrious Prison de la Santé (2nd division cell No. 48, Judge Delalé). Their obscene quality is acknowledged by all writers on Utrillo. These women loitering on the cobbled street that leads to Saint-Etienne-du-Mont are purveyors of the sort of love that can be acquired for a small sum; their sexuality is exalted and almost deified by the painter's fevered imagination. These identical, schematic prostitutes have much in common with prehistoric fertility idols or the simplified Eves that one finds in French Apocalypses of the eleventh century. Can Utrillo, spiritual brother of Goha-le-Simple, be considered the legitimate descendant of Aurignacian stone-cutters and Romanesque scribes?

The obsessions of a solitary artist gave birth to these mythical and sacrilegious images which bourgeois susceptibilities could not condone. During the 35 years which were left to him in which to pray and find his own peace, Utrillo oscillated between a soft moist technique and a rigorously linear graphic style.

22

An attempt at Psychoanalysis

Utrillo was not a psychopath, nor a retarded personality, nor a victim of dementia praecox. And the regression towards childish and precultural forms which characterises his work is in no sense analogous with the spiritual evolution of Gauguin who turned his back on the heritage of the High Renaissance and took his inspiration from the early beginnings of art. His orientation towards the images of primitive savage tribes was accidental and involuntary. This return to primitive sources is one of the dominant characteristics of twentieth century art (it marks the same evolution from one state to another as that which archaeologists tell us characterises remote antiquity).

If, as Freud himself admits, psychoanalysis is unable to explain the source of the creative power of a painter or a poet, a psychoanalytical investigation can nevertheless throw some light onto Utrillo's personality. Such an analysis should not refer to a study of Utrillo's favourite subjects. This would yield few results. Apart from a few still lifes, Utrillo was exclusively a painter of landscapes of Paris or other parts of France. It would certainly be absurd to interpret this choice of motifs as an expression of that mysterious illness doctors call claustrophobia. Charles Beaudouin, author of *Psychanalyse de l'Art,* on which the terminology of the present article is based, has already made the experiment.

What are the direct and indirect causes of Utrillo's mental unbalance? He was an illegitimate child. He had no contact with the man who was supposed to be his father. Suzanne Valadon entrusted the baby to Mme. Coulon. Her own life was irregular, the boy did not go back to her until he could walk and talk. Thus both in school and out of school the anomalies of his position were bound to attract attention. It is easy to suppose that this made a deep impression on him. The reaction to this trauma soon began to be visible. Affected by this first complex, the schoolboy, who felt his inferiority, became a rebel. Grandmother Coulon, also known as Maman Madeleine, found him surly and undisciplined. He drummed his feet, broke dishes and screamed whenever she opposed his wishes. Suzanne Valadon's lover, Paul Mousis, irrupted suddenly into his life. He represented authority and although always kindly disposed

"Le Lapin Agile" (*charcoal drawing*)

towards him, he remained in Utrillo's eyes the stranger who had power over his mother and who imposed his will on everyone. It was Paul Mousis who was responsible for making him go to school in Paris, found him a job in a bank, and then, seeing that his health was getting worse, arranged for him to go into a clinic. When his mother decided to leave Mousis and marry Utter, his hostility to the father-figure increased. As a child, Utrillo transferred his hatred, more or less repressed, of the head of the family, to the teachers at his secondary school in Paris. As a young man he rebelled against his employers. Later, his animosity was turned towards policemen, as exercising or personifying power. But this hatred of authority, this refusal to accept restraint, this contempt for the law are only a ramification and a symptom of the Œdipus complex. Utrillo's mother fixation made him a rebel not only against the inimical forces that came between him and his mother but also all their collaterals. The father, or pseudo-father, the schoolmaster, the director of the bank all stood for the same idea; they were superiors, hierarchical powers. The women in whom he subsequently became interested were all virile types who dominated him, like Suzanne Valadon had dominated him when he was a child. None of Utrillo's biographers state whether or not he had a Christian upbringing, the dates of his Baptism and First Communion are not known. We do not know at what point his religious feeling became a positive force. What we do know is that his need to blame is a moral reflex of religious origin. By repressing an impure desire he set in motion in his unconscious the guilt complex and the need for self-punishment which were to manifest themselves in various ways.

No one takes much notice of the story of the policemen who, when they took him back to his mother's house in Montmartre with a fractured skull (or jaw), claimed that he had tried to kill himself by throwing himself against a wall. Yet this explanation is perfectly plausible.

Utrillo's melancholy shows itself not only in the laziness and indifference which his mother tried to correct by turning his attention to painting. It is revealed in secondary complexes of degradation and abasement. The young man who destroyed himself so scientifically, kept low company and plumbed the depths of what is politely called a mental health centre. Was his chronic alcoholism a supreme attempt to escape? Or has it, on the contrary, a mystical basis? "He painted in order to drink and drank in order to paint," wrote one of the critics who knew him best. For Utrillo, alcohol was not simply a means

The painter with his spaniel Bicon in his villa at Le Vésinet

of satisfying his thirst; it was a philtre that gave him creative power, a divine nectar like the Hindu *Soma* which represents the spirit of strength. This elixir translated him to a state of otherness in which his vital forces were increased tenfold.

Art, according to Utrillo, is a means of satisfying those desires which one cannot exercise. It has considerable therapeutic value. It is a transference and a derivation. Yet it is necessary, as the psychologists affirm, that the aesthetic sublimation be present in its embryo state: it cannot be wholly induced...

Utrillo clearly is a misfit. He is not a paranoiac isolated in his madness and his solitude. When his feeling mechanism is disturbed, he resolves his conflicts and overcomes his suffering through the medium of art. The poet, says Charles Beaudouin, is his own doctor. So is the painter. In Utrillo's life art has the function of a purification: it is an Aristotelian catharsis.

WALDEMAR GEORGE

Although I knew and visited Utrillo before and during the first World War, I have also consulted the numerous studies devoted to the artist. The most reliable are those of Tabarant, Heuzé, Carco, Gustave Coquiot. Mention should also be made of the exhaustive studies of Robert Rey, Charensol, J. G. Gros. The theories of Utrillo's biographers, far from agreeing with each other, are contradictory. I have followed that of Tabarant. I should like to state here how much I owe to this enlightened critic. Finally, in the section, "An Attempt at Psychoanalysis," I have applied to Utrillo's case the principles followed by Charles Beaudouin in his work "Psychanalyse de l'Art."

W. G.

Plates

PLATE 1 - THE CHURCH OF SAINT-SEVERIN (detail)

Before the Church of Saint-Severin, should one recall Le Corbusier's book Quand les cathédrales étaient blanches? *The unpolished stone of Ile-de-France has been captured and expressed by a painter whose integrity equalled that of the masons who assembled it.*

PLATE 1 - THE CHURCH OF SAINT-SEVERIN. *National Gallery of Art Washington, D.C. (Chester Dale Collection)*

PLATE 2 - STREET IN PARIS (detail)

The perspective of this Paris street evokes, and justly so, the urban scenes that date from the first Italian Renaissance the modest Maurice Utrillo, perhaps without realising it, joins here the smaller masters of Quattrocento, who were painters and witnesses of their times.

PLATE 2 - STREET IN PARIS (1914). *Helen Birch Bartlett Memorial Collection* (Courtesy of The Institute of Chicago)

PLATE 3 - CHURCH IN PARIS (detail)

*This is but one church among many churches. Did Utrillo pray
in this venerable country church? He has painted it with a love
and a peaceful contemplation that are in themselves acts of faith.*

PLATE 3 - CHURCH IN PARIS. *Collection, The Museum of Modern Art, New York*

PLATE 4 - VIEW OF MONTMAGNY (detail)

Painted c. 1903. All sense of tragedy is absent from this radiant Ile-de-France landscape which forms a point of light in the painter's total work. The technique is based on a series of round or oblong brush-strokes. The actual working of the surface is reminiscent of Camille Pissarro.

PLATE 4 - VIEW OF MONTMAGNY (1903). *Private collection, Basle, Switzerland*

PLATE 5 - RUE ANDRÉ DEL SARTE, PARIS (detail)

Utrillo uses thick impasto. His moving Paris landscape is one of the high spots in the history of French painting. His technique owes much to Daubigny and Gustave Courbet. Anecdotic or descriptive factors are eliminated. The figures in the street are mere strokes of colour indicated with a flick of the brush. But all the objects preserve their three-dimensional quality.

PLATE 5 - RUE ANDRÉ DEL SARTE, PARIS (before 1912). *Private collection, Basle, Switzerland*

PLATE 6 - CAFÈ IN THE RUE MULLER, MONTMARTRE (detail)

A combination of rich colours and a summary, almost elliptical execution. Utrillo's technique is a form of shorthand. Yet there is nothing abstract or cerebral about it. On the contrary, it conveys a powerful impression of life. This view of Paris, the city celebrated by so many poets, is like a snapshot, but one which has the power to awake lyrical echoes in the mind of the spectator.

PLATE 6 - CAFÉ IN THE RUE MULLER, MONTMARTRE (before 1912). *Museum, Berne, Switzerland*

PLATE 7 · VILLAGE STREET IN THE ILE-DE-FRANCE (detail)

Utrillo simplifies his manner. His vision becomes clearer. He establishes his picture planes more trenchantly. Only the trees, with their feathery leaves outlined against the sky, indicate his connections with Impressionism.

PLATE 7 - VILLAGE STREET IN THE ILE-DE-FRANCE

PLATE 8 - HOUSE IN THE SUBURBS OF PARIS (detail)

Utrillo's artistic personality is becoming more freely defined, his vision more instinctive, more immediate, more uncompromising.

PLATE 8 - HOUSE IN THE SUBURBS OF PARIS (c. 1910). *Museum of Fine Arts, Berne, Switzerland*

PLATE 9 - LE LAPIN AGILE (detail)

The fence in the foreground serves as a foil for the painting.
An outstandingly humane picture.

PLATE 9 - LE LAPIN AGILE. *Dr. Giovanni Mattioli collection, Milan*

PLATE 10 - STREET ON THE BUTTE, MONTMARTRE (detail)

A very broadly painted canvas. The ground is streaked with colours dashed in with irregular strokes of the brush. There are traces of plaster on the walls of the houses and the palissade.

PLATE 10 - STREET ON THE BUTTE, MONTMARTRE

PLATE 11 - A CROSS-ROADS IN MONTMARTRE (detail)

In tracing the signs of hotels and bars on the walls of his shoddy houses, Utrillo might almost be said to join up with the Cubists. Certain historians consider him to be their precursor.

PLATE 11 - A CROSS-ROADS IN MONTMARTRE. *Dr. Guido Cavallini collection, Milan*

PLATE 12 - THE SEINE, PARIS (detail)

In this masterly and very early work Utrillo shows himself to
be the equal of the young Van Gogh. The schematic figure of
the boatman is modelled in paint laid on with a trowel. The
barge and quay are painted in local colours. A golden light
soffoses the sky and water.

PLATE 12 - THE SEINE, PARIS (1905). *Private collection, Basle, Switzerland*

It will hardly be necessary to remind readers that the Moulin de la Galette was a dance-hall in Montmartre frequented by painters, writers and local inhabitants. It was there that Renoir painted the large picture now in the Louvre and considered to be one of his masterpieces.

PLATE 13 - LE MOULIN DE LA GALETTE. *Private collection, Milan*

PLATE 14 - A VILLAGE CHURCH (detail)

This church is not merely a pictorial motif. It represents an act of faith, a passport to heaven delivered by God to an artist with a pure heart but a body undermined by drink.

PLATE 14 - A VILLAGE CHURCH

As a town painter, is Utrillo the descendant of those Quattro-cento masters of perspective whose clear statements, unwavering outlines and expert architectural drawings reveal their early training? Or is he simply a self-taught artist who paints as effort-lessly as a bird sings?

PLATE 15 - HOUSES IN MONTMARTRE

PLATE 16 - SNOW IN MONTMARTRE (detail)

A winter landscape of crystalline purity which reminds one of snowscapes painted by Brueghel the Elder. The snow, which is tangible and convincing, is the dominant note in this outstanding picture.

PLATE 16 - SNOW IN MONTMARTRE. *Private collection, Milan*

PLATE 17 - BARRACKS AT COMPIÈGNE (detail)

The figures, the colours and the frontality of the scene ally Utrillo with the Douanier Rousseau. The legacy of Suzanne Valadon and the Impressionists has been abandoned. Utrillo confronts us with an illiterate style which was to inspire masterpieces and which was to be perhaps the instrument of his salvation.

PLATE 17 - BARRACKS AT COMPIÈGNE. *Dr. Luigi Bordoli collection, Milan*

PLATE 18 - STREET IN MONTMARTRE WITH THE MOULIN DE LA GALETTE
IN THE BACKGROUND (detail)

*This is a difficult picture to date. Probably from the end of
the Montmagny period (1903-7) or the white period after 1910.
The value of this canvas is in its exceptionally pleasing colour
combinations. Utrillo has a true eye; the chromatic range of
this popular realist is scarcely less subtle than that of Fouquet.*

PLATE 18 · STREET IN MONTMARTRE WITH THE MOULIN DE LA GALETTE IN THE BACKGROUND.
Luigi Silvera collection, Alassio

PLATE 19 · SNOW IN MONTMARTRE (detail)

One would like to place this study of a square in Montmartre, next to a Venetian scene by Carpaccio with its exotic figures of turbaned Turks.

PLATE 19 - SNOW IN MONTMARTRE. *Dr. Giovanni Falck collection, Milan*

PLATE 20 - BAL RESTAURANT (detail)

Is this landscape of Sannois painted from life? Or is it a memory of Montmartre? A ghostly Moulin de la Galette makes the second theory more likely. Whatever the explanation, it is a canvas of high quality. Utrillo combines an Impressionist (or pre-Impressionist) technique with that feeling for the nature of things that is his own particular contribution.

PLATE 20 · BAL RESTAURANT (Sannois). *Dr. Serafino Corbetta, Chiavenna*

PLATE 21 - STREET IN MONTMARTRE WITH THE DOME OF SACRÉ-CŒUR
IN THE BACKGROUND (detail)

Montmartre is Utrillo's domain. But Montmartre does not explain Utrillo. If we study this canvas we realise that the artist shows a disconcerting boldness. The crudely painted figures, shutters and walls form part of the same plastic system. The brush strokes or rather flourishes retain their independence over and above the objects they represent.

PLATE 21 - STREET IN MONTMARTRE WITH THE DOME OF SACRÉ-CŒUR IN THE BACKGROUND.
Private collection, Milan

PLATE 22 - SPRING IN MONTMARTRE (detail)

Painted c. 1910. This evocation of an early spring day in the suburb of an industrial town has the charm of a drawing by a primary school child. The colour harmonies of this picture which pre-figures l'art brut *bear witness to an extremely refined taste. The civilization reproduced by Utrillo is not the product of book-learning. It is a way of life.*

PLATE 22 - SPRING IN MONTMARTRE. *Dr. Antonio Mazzotta collection, Milan*

PLATE 23 - THE BASILICA OF SACRÉ-CŒUR (detail)

The basilica stands out at the end of a narrow street flanked by walls whose rough texture Utrillo has managed to convey without in any way intending to deceive the eye.

PLATE 23 · THE BASILICA OF SACRÉ-CŒUR. *Ernesto Bestagini collection, Milan*

PLATE 24 - LE MOULIN DE LA GALETTE (detail)

This is a difficult picture to date. Probably from the white
period, after 1910. This sketch, an explosion of brilliant colour,
is an expression of Utrillo's joy in painting.

PLATE 24 - LE MOULIN DE LA GALETTE. *Ernesto Bestagini collection, Milan*

PLATE 25 - STREET IN MONTMARTRE (detail)

*Probably painted during the white period, c. 1910. If the figures
of the women were not so integrated in the picture space, and
if the execution were drier and more staccato, one would be
tempted to date this picture c. 1918-1925.*

PLATE 25 · STREET IN MONTMARTRE. *Paolo Lampugnani collection, Milan*

PLATE 26 - THE CHURCH OF SAINT-BERNARD (AIN) (detail)

This country church is not mentioned in the guidebooks. But Utrillo paints it with love and devotion. It is summer. The women are going to Mass. The white-walled church scarcely stands on the ground and seems to float between earth and heaven.

PLATE 26 - THE CHURCH OF SAINT-BERNARD (AIN) (1935). *Giuseppe Chiesa collection, Milan*

PLATE 27 - CHÂTEAU AT ALLONJOIE (detail)

Utrillo seems to have no feeling for the soil. His country scenes are fruitless attempts to escape. If he sometimes has recourse to picture postcards, these serve to orientate him and serve as signposts. These mediocre documents enable him to make admirable imaginary journeys.

PLATE 27 · CHÂTEAU AT ALLONJOIE. *Private collection, Rome*

PLATE 28 - THE GARDENS OF SACRÉ-CŒUR (detail)

Does this painting show artistic incompetence, ignorance or wilful disregard of the rules? Far from it, Utrillo's vision of the world is unique. His wondering eye is the eye of an illiterate who restores to art the sense of mystery and miracle.

PLATE 28 - THE GARDENS OF SACRÉ-CŒUR. *Private collection, Rome*

PLATE 29 - À LA BELLE GABRIELLE (detail)

Utrillo frequented Marie Vizier's cabaret before and during the first World War. It is therefore difficult to give a precise date to this picture which is painted with the vehemence of the Montmagny period. It is probably earlier than the picture reproduced on the following page.

PLATE 29 - À LA BELLE GABRIELLE (c. 1914). *Dr. Emilio Jesi collection, Milan*

PLATE 30 - ON THE CORNER OF LA BELLE GABRIELLE (detail)

The easy mastery of the Montmagny period has disappeared for good. The painter, who has discovered the effortless gift of seeing things through the eyes of a child, turns in on himself and returns to his sources. His art becomes a lesson in humility. Sometimes he shows similarities with Bosnian tomb graffiti or 9th century French illuminated manuscripts.

PLATE 30 - ON THE CORNER OF LA BELLE GABRIELLE. *Private collection, Milan*

PLATE 31 - THE CHURCH OF CRÈCHES-SUR-SAÔNE (detail)

This canvas is a typical example of craftsmanship pure and simple. It is true that craftsmanship here reaches a high level of perfection. The painter is no mere improvisor relying on inspiration. He works with a compass and ruler. He has a different technique for rendering stone, tiles, earth, foliage in the morning sunshine and a stretch of turquoise sky.

PLATE 31 - THE CHURCH OF CRÈCHES-SUR-SAÔNE

PLATE 32 - QUAI DE LA TOURNELLE (detail)

The painter's desire to reproduce exactly the inscriptions on the walls stretches realism to its limits. But this realism retains an extremely conceptual character. One wonders if one would be wise to trust it. Reality here slips through the net of curiosity and verges on fiction.

PLATE 32 - QUAI DE LA TOURNELLE (1915). *Private collection, Basle, Switzerland*

PLATE 33 - A COUNTRY CHURCH (detail)

This work is characteristic of Maurice Utrillo's last conscious researches. The handwriting is typical of a so-called "primitive" artist. His drawing has the sharpness of a medieval print, forming a contrast with the free pictorial handling of the vegetation.

PLATE 33 - A COUNTRY CHURCH (1922). *Private collection, Milan*

PLATE 34 - RUE DE LA FONTAINE À MULARD (detail)

Is this gypsy scene a pendant to the canvas which Van Gogh painted at Arles near the Pont de Trinquetaille? It sums up the painter's miserable and enchanted world, his vernacular style, his feeling for human beings vowed to poverty.

PLATE 34 - RUE DE LA FONTAINE À MULARD (1925). *Dr. Bernocchi collection, Milan*

PLATE 35 · **THE CHÂTEAU DE CHILLON** (detail)

A typical example of a Utrillo painted from a picture postcard. The theme is conventional, the composition and colour remind one of a tradesman's calendar. Apart from this, the painter tries to translate the image to a higher level.

PLATE 35 - **THE CHÂTEAU DE CHILLON** (1915-6). *Private collection, Zurich, Switzerland*

Index

14 *A village Church*

15 *Houses in Montmartre*

16 *Snow in Montmartre.* Private collection, Milan

17 *Barracks at Compiègne.* Dr. Luigi Bordoli collection, Milan

18 *Street in Montmartre with the Moulin de la Galette in the Background.* Luigi Silvera collection, Alassio

19 *Snow in Montmartre.* Dr. Giovanni Falck collection, Milan

20 *Bal Restaurant* (Sannois). Dr. Serafino Corbetta, Chiavenna

21 *Street in Montmartre with the Dome of Sacré-Cœur in the Background.* Private collection, Milan

22 *Spring in Montmartre.* Dr. Antonio Mazzotta collection, Milan

23 *The Basilica of Sacré-Cœur.* Ernesto Bestagini collection, Milan

24 *Le Moulin de la Galette.* Ernesto Bestagini collection, Milan

25 *Street in Montmartre.* Palo Lampugnani collection, Milan

26 *The Church of Saint-Bernard (Ain)* (1935. Giuseppe Chiesa collection, Milan

27 *Château at Allonjoie.* Private collection, Rome

28 *The gardens of Sacré-Cœur.* Private collection, Rome

29 *À la belle Gabrielle* (c. 1914). Dr. Emilio Jesi collection, Milan

30 *On the corner of la belle Gabrielle.* Private collection, Milan

31 *The Church of Crèches-sur-Saône*

32 *Quai de la Tournelle* (1915). Private collection, Basle, Switzerland

33 *A country church* (1922). Private collection, Milan

34 *Rue de la Fontaine à Mulard* (1925). Dr. Bernocchi collection, Milan

35 *The Château de Chillon* (1915-6). Private collection, Zurich, Switzerland

THE PRINTING AND OTHER PRODUCTION
OF THIS BOOK WAS EXECUTED AT D'ARTI
GRAFICHE DI AMILCARE PIZZI IN MILAN